To my favorite person
in the whole world.
I love you, Xavier.
Always.
Dad (S.A.J)

To my wonderful boys
I love your spirit, your smile,
and the love we share.
Mom (G.B)

for
Jax and Jaid and Xavi

FIRST EDITION
10 9 8 7 6 5 4 3 2 1

Stranger Comics | Los Angeles, CA

Printed in Hong Kong
100% Recycled Paper

strangerkids.com
Stranger Kids is a division of Stranger Comics

STRANGER
K I D S

presents

Children being raised by parents who do
not live together – whether because of divorce or
otherwise – oftentimes face conflicting emotions. If I love
one parent more will the other one be hurt? Is it alright to enjoy
different things with each parent? May I feel happy when there's
tension between my folks? These questions might be most visible if the
parents are recently separated, but children may continue to wrestle with
their feelings for years to come. As well, most if not all of us know and
love children in separate homes. *I Am Living in 2 Homes* describes in simple
and beautiful language the feelings children may have as their lives involve
two separate homes. The poem reinforces the idea that love, support and
consistency matter more to children than a mailing address (or two).

*I Am Living in 2 Homes is an essential book for all
families, especially those in this particular situation.*

~ Dr. Charles J. Sophy, FACN
(The Dr. Phil Show)

i am Living in 2 HOMES

written by

Garcelle Beauvais & Sebastian A. Jones

illustrated by

James C. Webster

art direction & storyboards
Darrell May

concept art
James C. Webster - Darrell May - Davida Benefield - Paul Davey

design & production art
Adrienne Sangastiano

editorial
Joshua Cozine

i am living in two homes
with my twin brother Jay.

I am living in two very different homes.

Mom,

She likes nature, the mountains and trees.

Rivers to splash in
up to your knees.

I am all things bold, fun-loving free.

And wonderfully loved.

When I go to school I get asked serious things. **Like**

You don't live with both your Mom and your Dad.
Don't you feel frustrated, guilty, and sad?

I say

I felt I'd done something so awfully wrong.

Until love from my Mommy,
so open and strong...

...embraced me.

When Jay and I go to Mommy's house,
She says

"Be at peace, my gentle loves,
my favorite people under heaven above.

"It's a grownup choice,
through no fault of your own,
your Dad and I are happier...

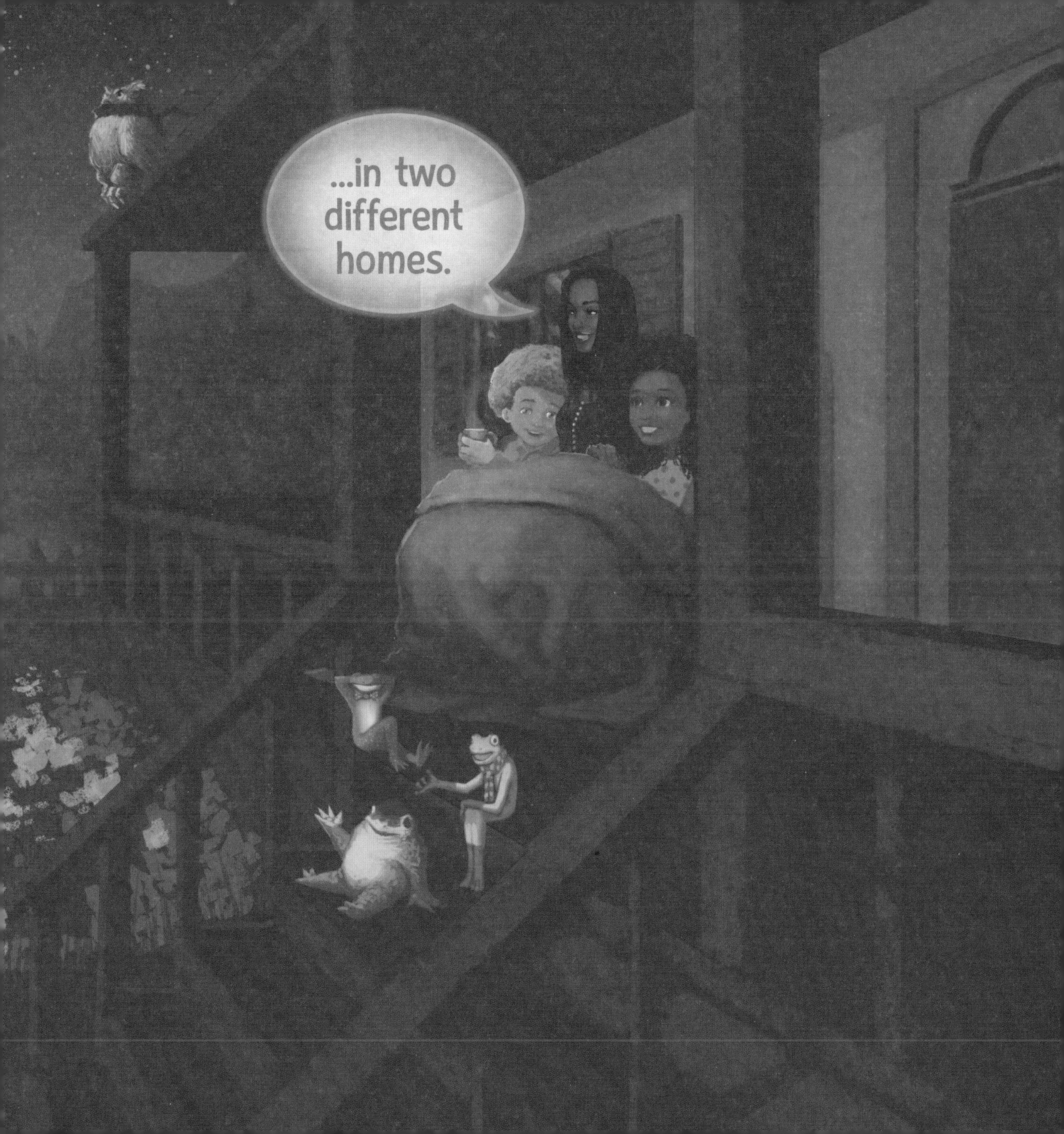
...in two different homes.

i am living in two homes
with my twin sister Nia.

I am living in two very different homes.

Dad,

He likes the city, bright lights and cars.
Trains that whistle both near and afar.

I am all things patient, careful, and calm.

And wonderfully loved.

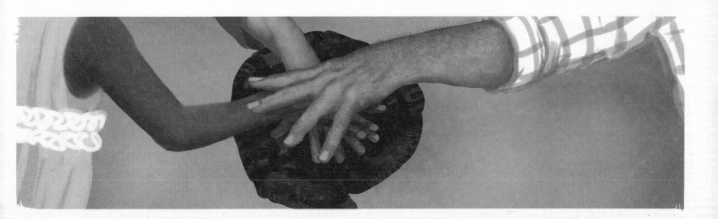

When I go to sleep I think of serious things. **Like**

Will Mommy and Daddy be married again?
Will I be forgotten if they make new friends?

I cried

in my bed feeling scared and confused.

Until love from my Daddy,
so honest and true...

...protected me.

When Nia and I go to Daddy's house,
He says

"It's okay to cry and shout to the wind.
Stomp it out, don't keep it all in.

"But know that we love you
and you're never alone.
Many families live...

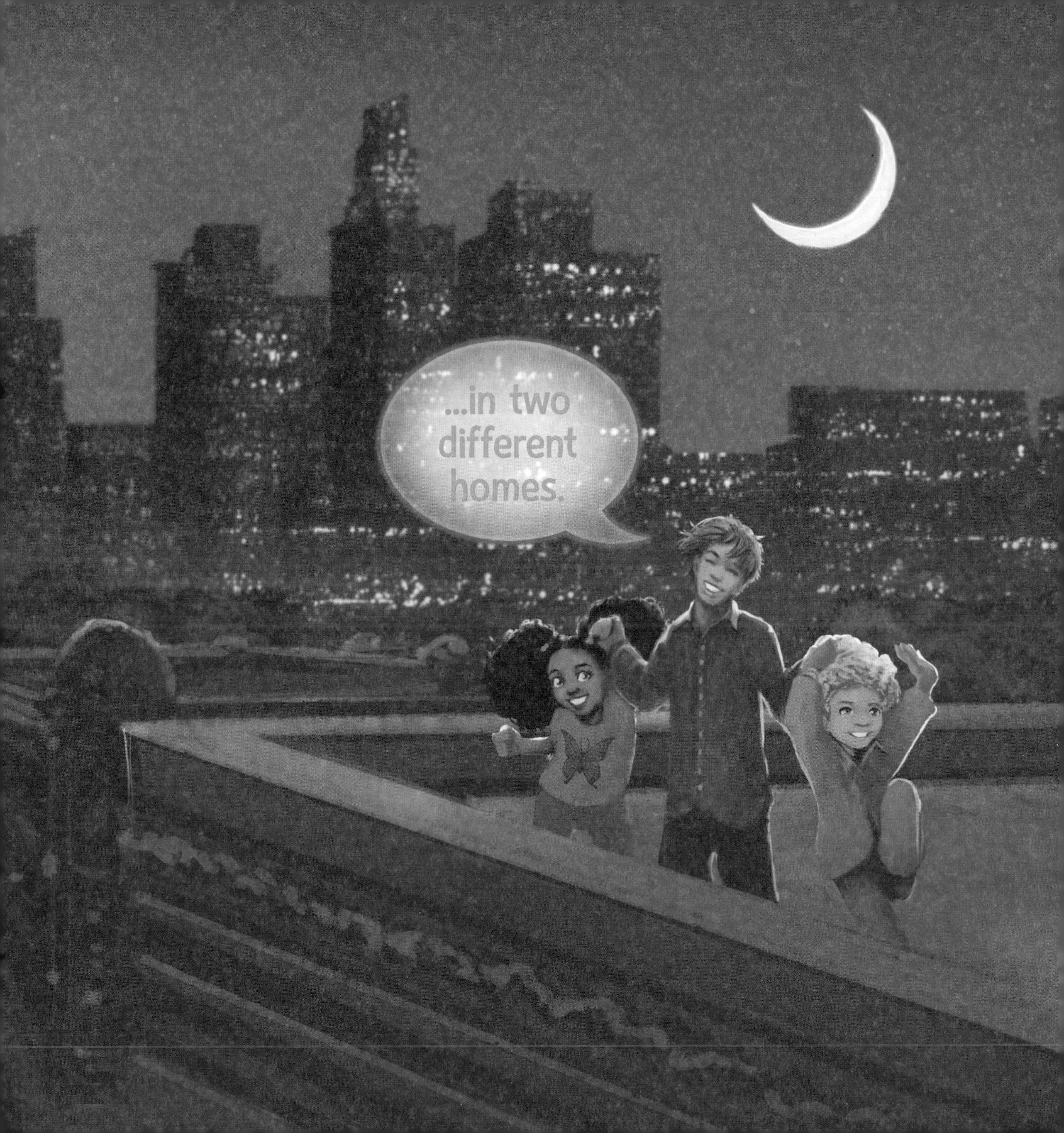
...in two different homes.

i am making the best of having two homes.
With Mom I go fishing, make dandelion chains.

With Dad I watch movies,
                have adventures and games.

It's hard for my parents,
this feels very new.

They will make mistakes,
            and I know I will too.

So I will clean up my room,
help out and pitch in.

Get to know them each better,
and to them I will sing...

Don't show me your anger, I'm only a kid.
Just read me a story...

And please tuck me in.

Ice cream won't fix this, treats or new toys.

Quality time together,
        loving each other, whatever the weather...

...is what I most enjoy!

Love is LOVE.

Family is FAMILY.

i am LiViNG iN 2 HOMES

There are people all over the world who have families that live in **different homes**. Many kids live with either their Mom or Dad, but not at the same time. Some have stepmoms and stepdads. Others live with grandparents. All families are different, and they love each other with all their hearts. There is no right or wrong. Just remember to be happy and thankful for your family, because you can live in one home or two, or maybe even more, but all that matters is...

Love is LOVE. Family is FAMILY.

about me...

My name is _____ .

I am _____ years old.

I have _____ brother(s) and _____ sister(s).

I was born in _____ .

My favorite song is _____ .

My favorite food is _____ .

My home or homes are in _____ .

My favorite places to play in my home(s) are _____ and

_____ .

When I go from one home to the other I feel _____ .

If I ever feel lonely, I _____ .

The best part about living in different homes is _____

because _____ !

Draw Jay's Treehouse!

Draw Nia's Treehouse!

A note for parents:

After sharing *I Am Living in 2 Homes* with your child,
you can use these discussion questions to help start a conversation
about your living situation, both the difficulties and the
opportunities for a happy life.

1. How is your family similar/different from Jay and Nia's family? What makes your family special?

2. What is the best part about living in different homes? What is the most difficult part?

3. When Nia is at school, she is asked, "You don't live with both your Mom and your Dad. Don't you feel frustrated, guilty, and sad?" Have you ever had these feelings? What can you do if you're feeling this way? (If your child is unsure, talk about how Nia's mom helps her feel better. A hug is always a good remedy! It's also important to talk about your thoughts and emotions with a loved one.)

4. What are some of the serious things that Jay thinks about when he goes to bed? What are some of the serious things that you think about sometimes?

5. What can you do if you are feeling alone?

6. Nia and Jay enjoy quality time separately with each parent. What do you enjoy doing with your loved ones?

See more from the *I Am* book series at

strangerkids.com

Originally from England, **Sebastian** founded the critically acclaimed MVP records at 18, turning his love of American roots music into a business. More recently, he created Stranger Comics to do the same with his love of fanciful tales and quality escapism. Sebastian is honored to celebrate the *I Am* book series with his son, Xavier.

Stranger Comics
educational director
Megan Lewitin
marketing
Eddie DeAngelini
Hannibal Tabu
Tabitha Grace Smith
development
Mike Hodge
Christopher Garner
digital supervisor
Ken Locsmandi
art director
Darrell May
editor-in-chief
Joshua Cozine
publisher
Sebastian A. Jones

Born to create, **James** is a menagerie of artistic expression, interpretation and execution. Classically trained by an array of talented professors at Syracuse University, James has been working with the Stranger team since 2011. He currently resides in Atlanta with his extremely talented and brilliant lady, Adrienne, the designer and production artist for the *I Am* book series.

Garcelle is Haitian born and immigrated to the United States at the age of seven. She has since charmed audiences with her dramatic and comedic abilities in both television and film. Always wanting to give back, Garcelle is active with charities including Step Up Women's Network, March of Dimes, and EDEYO, a Haitian children's organization. In addition to writing children's books, she has a popular blog on People.com focusing on parenting and all things women. Garcelle lives in Los Angeles, where she is happiest spending time with her sons, Oliver and the twins, Jax and Jaid, who were the inspiration for the series.

We would like to thank

Paul Almond, TC Badalato, Marie Beaubien, Marie Claire Beauvais, The Bergtings, Kami Broyles, Andrew Cosby, Elena Cunningham, Dawn Eyers, Jennifer Foutch, Kristina Gravely, Jennifer Green, Mark & Katie Hammond, Mark Hovanec, Gray Jones, Noel Johnson, Lloyd Levin, Bob Lieberman, Mona Loring, Norma McCandless, Kristen Merlene, Omilaju Miranda, Craig Pollock, Indira Salazar, Oliver Saunders, Diane Simowski, Sonia Smith-Kang, Dr. Sophy, Andrew Sugerman, Tim Taylor, Rose Tinker, Lori-Ann & Jens Quast, Elizabeth Ricin, David Uslan and Luke Whitehead